MINDFUL ME
GET OUTDOORS

A Mindfulness Guide
to Noticing Nature

Written by
Paul Christelis

Illustrated by
Elisa Paganelli

W
FRANKLIN
WATTS

WHAT IS MINDFULNESS?

Mindfulness is a way of paying attention to our present moment experience with an attitude of kindness and curiosity. Most of the time, our attention is distracted – often by thoughts about the past or future – and this can make us feel jumpy, worried, self-critical and confused.

By gently moving our focus from our busy minds and into the present moment, we begin to let go of distraction and learn to tap into the ever-present supply of joy and ease that resides in the here-and-now. Mindfulness can also help us to improve concentration, calm unpleasant emotions, even boost our immune systems.

In this book, children are encouraged to cultivate mindfulness by becoming curious about the natural world around them. By placing attention on their environment, they can quieten their distracted, worried or self-critical minds.

Focusing on nature also reminds us that we are intrinsically connected to the wider world, which can make us feel more secure and can instil empathy for all living creatures and a sense of responsibility for the impact we make on the environment.

The book can be read interactively, allowing readers to pause at various points and bring their attention to what they are noticing. The in the text suggests where you might encourage readers to be curious about what they observe, whether this is outdoors, indoors, or an internal response to what they see, hear, smell, etc. Each time this is used, mindfulness is deepened. Don't rush this pause; really allow enough time for children to stay with their experience.

It doesn't matter if what they feel or notice is pleasant or unpleasant: what's important is to pay attention to it with a friendly attitude. This will introduce them to a way of being in the world that promotes health and happiness.

It's Saturday morning and Jada and her brother Michael are watching TV.

"That's all they ever do!" sighs their dad.

"It's a **beautiful** day and we are lucky enough to have a garden, but they won't budge from that couch!"

Suddenly, Dad has an idea. "Kids, who wants to win a **prize**?"
This gets their attention: "Me! Me!" they both shout.
"Then switch off the TV and listen up!"

"You're going to play the Garden Game. The winner is the person who can notice the most **interesting** things in the garden. Take a notebook each, and a pen, to write down everything you see. And remember: sometimes the smallest things are the most interesting. So observe carefully!"

"What's the prize?" asks Michael, who is very competitive.

"It's a **surprise**," says Dad. "Now off you go. You have until midday."

Do you have a garden or a park near your home? Take a moment to be curious about how much time you spend indoors and how long you spend outdoors.

👆 ▶ PAUSE BUTTON

"Hmm," moans Jada, looking at the garden. "There's not that much that's interesting here. All I see are the usual flowers and grass."

"Try slowing down and looking more closely," suggests Dad. "Sometimes, things that are worth noticing take time to see clearly."

Let's take a peek at some of Michael's discoveries. Like Jada, he also sees flowers. But he **notices** so many different types!

flower with white petals
red flowers
yellow petals with green edges
purple flowers
small pink flowers

11

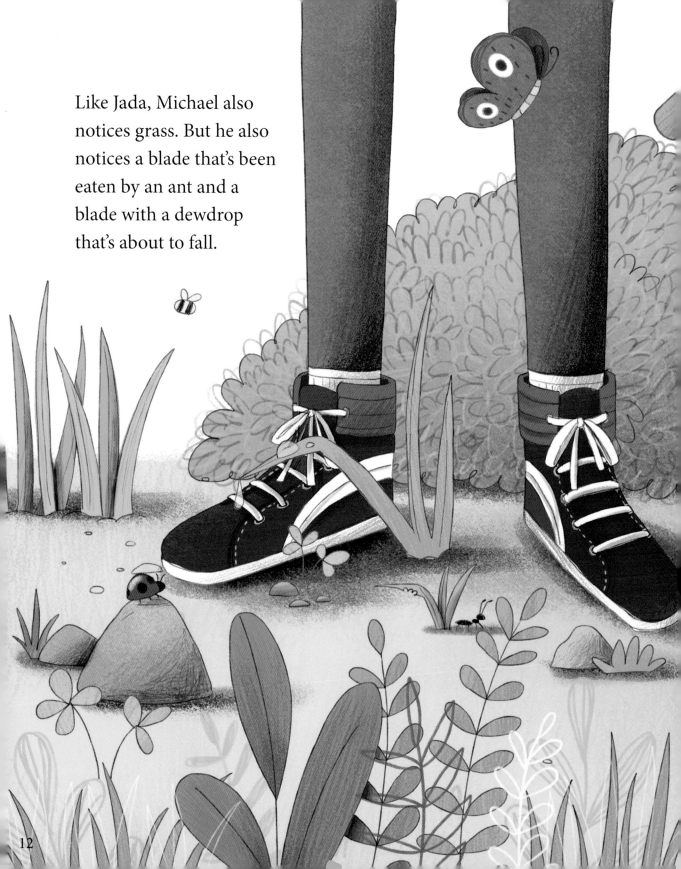

Like Jada, Michael also notices grass. But he also notices a blade that's been eaten by an ant and a blade with a dewdrop that's about to fall.

It's as if Michael's eyes have become magnifying glasses!

You can also turn your eyes into magnifying glasses! All you have to do is to decide to look at things slowly and to be really curious about what you're looking at. Try it now: choose an object close by and spend some time looking at it carefully. Name all the small details that make this object unique.

👆 PAUSE BUTTON

Jada tries looking at the grass with **curiosity** and this is what she sees:

FLOWERS

PAW PRINTS

A LADYBIRD

FOOTPRINTS

14

Dad shouts out from the kitchen:
"Looking with your eyes is one way of taking notice
of what's around you. But it's not the only way!"
Jada and Michael are puzzled. How else can they take notice?

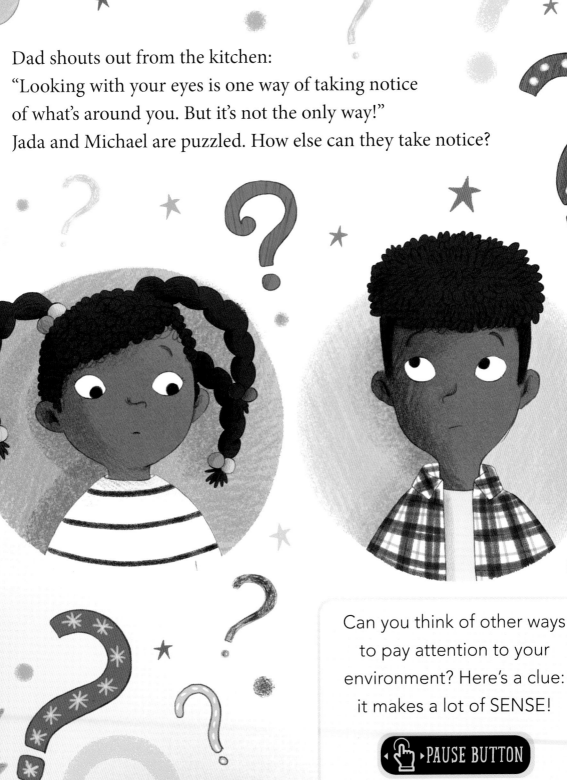

Can you think of other ways
to pay attention to your
environment? Here's a clue:
it makes a lot of SENSE!

▸ PAUSE BUTTON

We notice by seeing, smelling, tasting, touching and hearing; our five **senses**. Sometimes one sense is stronger, sometimes another. When we use our senses to pay attention the whole world opens up for us in interesting ways!

Right now, Jada's using her sense of touch; she's kneeling on a wet clump of grass and her knees feel cold and a little itchy. "That's a good observation to write down!" she thinks.

Jada moves to a warmer, drier part of the garden.
Her cold knees slowly begin to feel like muffins being
warmed in an oven. She seldomly notices her knees.
It feels good to notice them now!

Michael pauses to notice his sense of **touch** too. The soft, moist grass cools his bare feet. There's an ant crawling over his elbow – it feels a little prickly!

What do you notice right now with your sense of touch? Your clothes against your skin? Your fingers on the page of this book? Being patient and curious will make this sense more powerful, so don't rush your noticing.

PAUSE BUTTON

"What happens when I switch to **hearing**?" wonders Jada. She moves her attention to her ears and listens ...

At first, all she can hear is birdsong ...

… but then she remembers to be patient and curious. She closes her eyes which makes the sense of hearing even sharper.

Wow! So many other sounds begin to appear …

… And if she listens even closer, she can tune into the **silence** in-between sounds!

What sounds can you discover right now? All you need to do is close your eyes for about a minute, relax, and patiently wait for sounds to appear. You don't have to try to hear them: let the sounds come to you! Say to yourself, "Welcome Sounds! I'm ready to hear you!" And if all you hear is silence, then let yourself listen to that.

PAUSE BUTTON

23

While Jada is listening to sounds, Michael is on all fours at the other end of the garden. Dad sees him from the kitchen window. "Is he pretending to be a dog?" he wonders.

With his nose in the flower bed,
Michael is using his sense of **smell**
to discover many different scents given off
by the flowers: some smell sweet like honey,
others don't have a strong aroma …

… and then, a strong, almost spicy,
smell that makes his whole face
frown. Ugh! The neighbour's
dog has been using the flower
bed for a toilet!

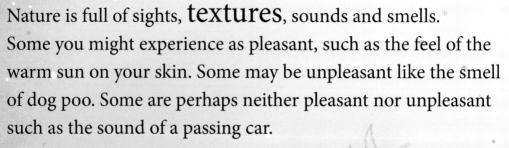

Nature is full of sights, textures, sounds and smells. Some you might experience as pleasant, such as the feel of the warm sun on your skin. Some may be unpleasant like the smell of dog poo. Some are perhaps neither pleasant nor unpleasant such as the sound of a passing car.

Just imagine what it would be like if we didn't have
our senses to experience the world around us!
We wouldn't notice very much, would we?

So take a moment
right now to really appreciate
each of your senses.
- What do you see?
- What do you hear?
- What do you notice with your
sense of touch?
- Can you smell anything?

"Wait a moment!" says Michael. "We've forgotten something!"
Jada realises this too. "What is it?" She can almost remember.
"It's on the tip of my tongue …"

Can you remember what Jada and Michael have forgotten? It's on the tip of your TONGUE too!

PAUSE BUTTON

"Time for your surprise!" Jada's dad calls. They run into the kitchen, leaving their notebooks on the grass.

"That's it!" the children shout, feeling their mouths begin to water at the sight of delicious, sweet cake. "Our sense of **taste**!"

SWEET

Who cares about a competition when there are so many senses to savour!

CREAMY

RASPBERRY

NOTES FOR PARENTS AND TEACHERS

Here are a few other mindfulness exercises and suggestions to add to your child's Mindful Toolkit. These are simple, effective and, above all, fun to do!

SENSES IN A BOX
You can play this game with as many players as you like. Write down each of the five senses on five pieces of paper, fold them and put them in a small box. When it's your turn, choose a piece of paper from the box. Read out the sense that's written on that paper. If, for example, you have picked SMELL, then set a timer for three minutes and during this time, all players should use their sense of smell to pay attention to what's around them. Write down all of your observations, just as Jada and Michael did in the story. At the end of the three minutes, spend some time sharing what you found. What was the most common smell? The most pleasant? Unpleasant? Unusual? Then choose a different player to pick a new sense from the box.

If you really want to sharpen your attention during this game, try playing it in silence. Talking can dilute our attention and distract us from noticing things.

This game is best played outdoors to take advantage of the endless wonders of nature around us. However, if it is not possible to be outside then exploring indoors can work well too. What's important is to remain curious and open to our environment, wherever we may be.

BE A TREE
This practice is a standing meditation that encourages stillness and receptivity to what's around us.

Choose a spot outside, preferably where there are trees present. Encourage children to stand upright, still and relaxed, just like a tree. They can imagine that they have roots growing from under their feet into the earth. They can spread their fingers and notice the feel of the breeze or wind moving through their hands, just like wind passing through tree branches. This is especially effective with closed eyes, allowing them to deeply experience the feeling of standing in the open, and allowing them to hear the sounds around them.

SUPER SENSE SPOT

A variation of the standing tree practice is to sit down and to claim that spot as your Super Sense Spot. Notice how it feels to make contact with the ground, then look around you and take in as many sights, smells and sounds as you can. Remember to look above at the sky and notice shapes and textures of cloud or the colour of blue, grey, etc.

Notice that if you sit for long enough you notice different things. In fact, it is important to really give yourself enough time for this because initially the first few minutes can seem unremarkable. It's only when we slow our attention right down that we start to pay attention to all the little sensations that are going on in and around us.

What's really great about all of these mindfulness practices is that there is no such thing as a right or wrong 'answer'. Simply allow your child to have his or her own response to stimuli. Help them to be curious about how they experience the world by entering into the experience with them: "Tell me more about that"; "How does that sunset make you feel inside?"; "What's it like to stand as still as a tree?". Share your own responses too – this teaches children to accept and validate others' experience, even if it differs from theirs.

FURTHER READING

Acorns to Great Acorns: Meditations for Children, Marie Delanote
(Findhorn Press Ltd, 2017)

Glad to be Dan: Discover How Mindfulness Helps Dan to Be Happy Every Day,
Jo Howarth and Jude Lennon (CreateSpace Independent Publishing Platform, 2016)

Master of Mindfulness: How to be Your Own Superhero in Times of Stress,
Laurie Grossman (New Harbinger, 2016)

Mindful Monkey, Happy Panda, Lauren Alderfer and Kerry Lee McLean
(Wisdom Publications, 2011)

Mindful Movements: Ten Exercises for Well-being, Wietske Vriezen
(Parallax Press, 2008)

Planting Seeds: Practicing Mindfulness with Children,
Thich Nhat Hanh (Parallax Press, 2011)

Sitting Still Like a Frog, Eline Snel
(Shambhala Publications Inc., 2014)

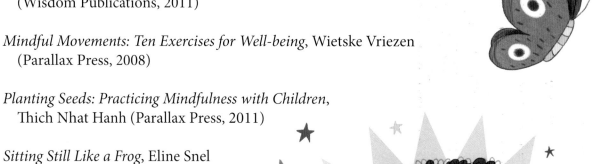